PUTTING
THE
PLANET
FIRST

ECO-CITIES

Nancy Dickmann

WAYLAND
www.waylandbooks.co.uk

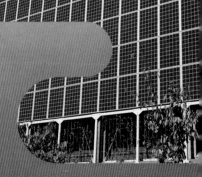

Published in paperback in Great Britain in 2019
by Wayland

Copyright © Hodder and Stoughton 2017

Editors: Paul Mason, Elizabeth Brent

Design: Peter Clayman

ISBN: 978 1 5263 0166 6

10 9 8 7 6 5 4 3 2

Wayland, an imprint of
Hachette Children's Group
Part of Hodder and Stoughton
Carmelite House
50 Victoria Embankment
London EC4Y 0DZ

An Hachette UK Company
www.hachette.co.uk
www.hachettechildrens.co.uk

Printed and bound in Dubai

Picture acknowledgements:
All images courtesy of Shutterstock except p5: TonyV3112/Shutterstock.com; p6–7: Joseph
Sohm/Shutterstock.com; p9: kah loong lee/Shutterstock.com; p12: Susan Montgomery/
Shutterstock.com; p15: TK Kurikawa/Shutterstock.com; p17: Igor Plotnikov/Shutterstock.com;
p21: Getty Images/Boston Globe; p23: Gallo Images – Neil Overy.

CONTENTS

WHAT IS AN ECO-CITY?

Do you live in a town or a city? Today, more than half of us do. One day soon, many city dwellers may be living in a new type of city: an eco-city.

The idea of an eco-city is that the people living there have a good quality of life, while using up as few natural resources as possible. These natural resources include food, water, energy and building materials.

Some older cities are making changes to become eco-cities. There are also some new cities that are being built from scratch as eco-cities.

People drive less in eco-cities, which helps the planet.

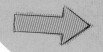

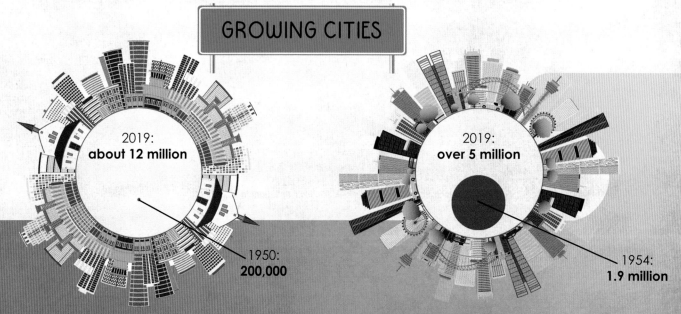

GROWING CITIES

2019:
about 12 million

1950:
200,000

Kinshasa, Democratic Republic of the Congo

2019:
over 5 million

1954:
1.9 million

Sydney, Australia

As the populations of cities grow, they use more and more resources.

HELPING THE PLANET

The world's population is growing, which is using up the planet's natural resources. If we use all the resources now, there will be none left for people in the future.

If people in the future are to have enough resources, we need to use fewer today. Eco-cities are designed so that people need to drive their cars less, and use less energy to heat and power their homes. These are ways of making urban life less harmful to the planet.

ECO-CITIES AND ECOSYSTEMS

The idea of an eco-city is based on a natural ecosystem. An ecosystem is a group of living things and the place where they live.

The parts of an ecosystem are connected together. For example, some plants in an ecosystem grow in soil. Animals eat these plants to live. When the animals die, bacteria and insects break them down. The animals then become part of the soil.

ECOSYSTEM CITIES

In a similar way to an ecosystem, all the parts of an eco-city – from transport and housing to parks and sewers – are designed to work together. Resources within the eco-city can provide its people with energy and food, rather than bringing these in from outside. The city's products can be re-used, recycled or burned to generate energy.

Features that make a city more eco-friendly:

| compact housing | public transport | green spaces | cycle paths | renewable energy | waste recycling |

BIOSPHERE 2

In 1991, a group of eight scientists in Arizona, USA, started an incredible experiment. They wanted to learn how to live in harmony within an ecosystem, in a similar way to residents of eco-cities.

The scientists went to live in a complex of glass buildings – an extreme version of an eco-city – for two years. The buildings, called Biosphere 2, were designed to re-create some of Earth's natural ecosystems, such as deserts, grasslands and tropical rainforests. Once inside, the scientists had no access to the outside world. They had to grow all their own food and generate their own power.

Research such as that done in Biosphere 2 informs the design of eco-cities.

ZERO-CARBON LIVING

One of the challenges facing eco-cities is to produce less of a gas called carbon dioxide (CO_2). Carbon dioxide damages the environment.

THE PROBLEM WITH CO_2

Carbon dioxide is released when we burn fossil fuels such as oil, coal or natural gas. It builds up in the atmosphere, where it traps heat. This is causing Earth's average temperature to rise. The result is climate change, with droughts and more extreme weather.

Many eco-cities would like to be zero-carbon cities. This means releasing no CO_2 into the air – easier said than done! Most of our energy comes from fossil fuels. Everything, from driving a car to charging a phone, releases CO_2.

CO_2 EMISSIONS PER HOUSEHOLD

Sweden
4.5 tonnes

China
7.5 tonnes

Australia
15.4 tonnes

World Bank statistics relating to carbon emissions, 2014. .

Petaling Jaya's population is growing, but the city is still determined to cut its total carbon emissions.

PETALING JAYA

There aren't currently any large cities that are truly zero-carbon, but many cities are working to reduce their carbon levels as much as possible.

The city of Petaling Jaya, in Malaysia, has made a plan to help reduce its CO_2 emissions by 30 per cent by the year 2030.

The plan includes using less electricity in homes and businesses, and installing cleaner ways of generating energy, such as solar panels on buildings (see pages 10 and 11). The city will also improve its public transport system, so that more people travel on buses instead of driving their cars, and install charging stations for electric cars.

GOING RENEWABLE

To avoid burning fossil fuels, which releases CO$_2$, eco-cities use other sources of energy, called 'renewables'.

Renewable energy comes from sources that will never run out, such as the Sun, wind or running water. These types of power produce very little CO$_2$, and cause far less harm to the environment than fossil fuels.

Sometimes, renewable energy can be generated within the eco-city itself, for example by solar panels on buildings, or wind turbines. Other times, an eco-city can get electricity from a solar power station in the countryside nearby, or from an offshore wind farm.

ECO-CITY ENERGY

Solar thermal power provides heat

City produces sewage and wastewater, and their heat is captured and re-used

Wind power provides electricity

Solar panels on homes and offices provide electricity

Power plants provide both electricity and heat

Water from seas, rivers and lakes provides natural cooling

City produces rubbish, which is burned to generate heat

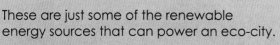
These are just some of the renewable energy sources that can power an eco-city.

One day soon, most new buildings might have solar panels built into their walls.

THE SOLAR WALL

Lots of people have installed solar panels on their roofs. But some architects are going one step further, and making solar panels part of the buildings themselves. They replace materials normally used for roofs, skylights or wall coverings with panels that can generate electricity.

In South Korea, one new office building has been built with a wall made of solar panels. They are special panels that shade the building's inside to keep it cool, but also let in daylight. At the same time, they generate about 10 per cent of the building's electricity.

URBAN DESIGN

No city can be zero-carbon if it still has thousands of cars on the roads. This is because most cars run on petrol or diesel fuel, which release CO_2 into the air.

In many cities, shops and offices are in the centre. Lots of people travel in from the edge of the city to work or go shopping. Others travel from one part of the city to another to go to school or work. If everyone makes these journeys by car, a lot of pollution is released.

New eco-cities are laid out so that people can get from place to place without using a car. Homes, shops, schools and offices are grouped close enough together that most residents can travel by walking or cycling.

In London, more than 610,000 bike journeys are made each day.

TRAVELLING TO WORK

In the UK, most people travel to work by car.

Car 72%

Train 11%

Bus 5%

Bicycle 3%

Walking 4%

Other 5%

LONDON: BIKE CITY

The local government in London, UK, wants more people to travel by bicycle. It has introduced two important schemes to encourage people to cycle.

First, London is building a network of 'cycle superhighways' that run from the edges of the city into the centre. These routes often follow main roads, but they have separate cycle paths. This makes cycling safer (one of the reasons many Londoners give for not cycling is that it is not safe).

London also has a bike-hire scheme. For a small fee, people can collect a bicycle at one docking station and return it to any other docking station once they have finished. There are over 10,000 bicycles available and more than 700 docking stations.

PUBLIC TRANSPORT

In bigger cities, some trips are too long to walk or cycle. If people drive cars for these journeys, it uses up fuel and releases CO$_2$. This is where public transport comes in.

Buses, trams and trains all help people to get where they need to go. When buses and trams have special lanes to cut through the traffic, they are also much faster than a car.

A bus or a train does use more fuel than a car, but it can carry many more passengers. This means a full bus or train uses far less fuel per person than a car. And many cities are upgrading their bus fleets, with buses that get some or all of their power from renewable electricity.

CARS VERSUS TRAMS

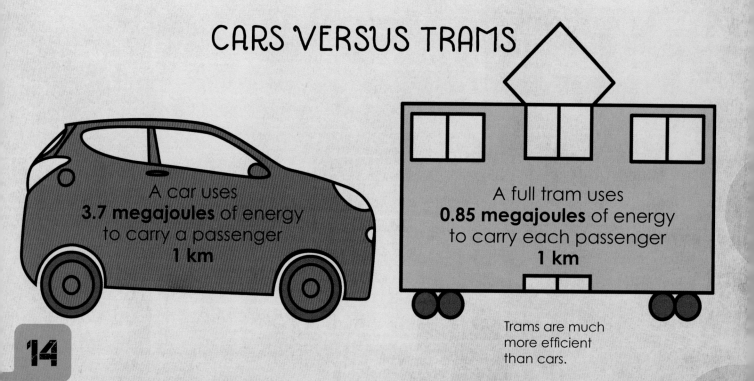

A car uses
3.7 megajoules of energy
to carry a passenger
1 km

A full tram uses
0.85 megajoules of energy
to carry each passenger
1 km

Trams are much more efficient than cars.

Electric tram in Melbourne, Australia.

TRAM-TASTIC MELBOURNE!

The city of Melbourne, in Australia, has the world's biggest tram network. Each year, more than 175 million tram journeys are made in the city.

Trams are like trains, but they run on tracks along city streets, instead of on separate train lines. The trams in Melbourne are electric, and they get their power from wires that run above the tram routes.

Melbourne is encouraging more people to use the trams, rather than travelling by car, by making some routes free. The tram system has more than 1,760 stops dotted across the city, so travelling by tram is quick and easy.

ECO-HOUSING

To make transport easier, eco-cities have to be compact. This often means that people live in blocks of flats instead of houses.

USING LESS ENERGY

Because flats are usually smaller than houses, it takes less energy to warm them up or cool them down. They also share walls, so once the whole building is warm or cool, less energy is needed to keep it at that temperature.

Homes in eco-cities are built with plenty of insulation, so they stay cool in summer and warm in winter. Some eco-homes make use of recycled or renewable building materials. These include straw bales, insulating foam made from seaweed, and even plastic 'wood' that is actually made from recycled carrier bags!

HOUSE SIZES

Average house sizes are very different from country to county. Bigger homes typically use more energy than small ones.

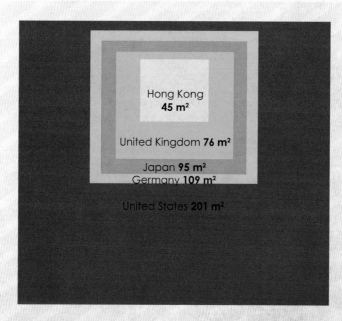

Hong Kong
45 m²

United Kingdom **76 m²**

Japan **95 m²**
Germany **109 m²**

United States **201 m²**

RECYCLED HOMES

In some places, people are recycling metal shipping containers and turning them into homes. The containers can be stacked on top of each other to make blocks of flats. They are compact and affordable, and don't use much energy. Re-using existing structures in this way saves natural resources.

In France, for example, shipping containers have been converted and stacked up to make housing for university students. Each container has a bathroom, living area and small kitchen. The containers have been arranged to leave space for walkways and balconies.

These shipping containers in France provide compact, efficient homes for students.

PUBLIC BUILDINGS

A building's carbon footprint refers to the total amount of CO_2 and other harmful gases it releases. Big buildings can have big carbon footprints.

Making large buildings more energy-efficient can help a city to reduce the total amount of CO_2 it releases. As a result, many cities have passed laws that require new buildings to be energy-efficient.

In France, for example, the government has deemed it unlawful for shops and office buildings to leave their lights on all night. Experts think this should save enough electricity to power 750,000 homes for a year.

POWERING BIG BUILDINGS

The type of energy used to power a building has a big effect on the amount of CO_2 it releases.

Using wind energy releases almost no CO_2.

Using natural gas releases 19 times as much CO_2 as wind energy.

Using coal releases 34 times as much CO_2 as wind energy.

From the top of the Reichstag's dome, visitors see an amazing view of Berlin.

GREEN PARLIAMENT

The Reichstag is an historic building in Berlin, Germany, dating back to 1894. It is where the country's parliament meets. In 1999, the Reichstag reopened after building work to make it more energy-efficient, and it now produces more energy than it uses.

A glass dome in the roof lets in natural light and heat, and can be opened for ventilation. The dome has a sun shield that tracks the Sun and blocks direct sunlight, to keep the building from getting too hot. Extra heat is used to warm fluid, which is then stored deep underground, and used for heating in the winter.

WASTE MANAGEMENT

Everything we no longer need – from an empty crisp packet or a pair of too-small jeans, to the grass clippings from your lawn – has to go somewhere.

LANDFILL PROBLEMS

In many cities, this rubbish gets collected and buried in landfills. But these take up valuable space, and there is so much waste, that finding places to put it is becoming a big problem. Also, as the waste decomposes, it releases greenhouse gases, which damage the environment.

REUSE AND RECYCLING

In an eco-city, waste is reused or recycled as much as possible. Cardboard boxes and aluminium drinks cans can be recycled into new products. Garden and food waste can be composted to make fertiliser. Some waste can be burned in power plants to generate electricity.

CUTTING DOWN ON RUBBISH

Between 1998 and 2015, Freiburg, in Germany, cut its non-recyclable waste by 85 per cent.

1998
140,000
tonnes
of rubbish

2015
20,623
tonnes
of rubbish

Displays at a Vermont museum teach visitors about recycling.

RECYCLING REVOLUTION

Until recently, only about 35 per cent of the waste produced in Vermont, USA, was recycled or composted. In 2012, the state government decided to change that.

They passed a law that made it illegal to throw away anything that could be recycled, such as cardboard, plastic bottles, garden waste or food scraps. Many areas of the state also introduced 'pay-as-you-throw' charges. With these, people are charged according to the amount of trash they throw out.

Although it costs money to throw out waste, recycling is free. This has made recycling as much as you possibly can a lot more popular.

SAVING WATER

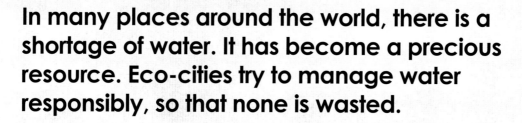

In many places around the world, there is a shortage of water. It has become a precious resource. Eco-cities try to manage water responsibly, so that none is wasted.

GREY WATER

One way of doing this is to recycle grey water. This is wastewater that comes from sinks, showers and washing machines. It is fairly clean, because it doesn't include any wastewater from toilets.

Grey water can be treated and then reused for toilet flushing or watering gardens. Because the water is used twice, this is more eco-friendly than using clean water from a tap or hosepipe.

WATER USE

Food and drink
6 litres

In the UK, each person uses 150 litres of water per day, on average, on these activities.

Washing clothes
19.5 litres

Toilet flushing
45 litres

Washing
49.5 litres

These colourful containers collect rainwater for drinking.

RECYCLING WATER

Ivory Park is a poor area near the city of Johannesburg, South Africa. An organisation called the EcoCity Trust has been working there to improve the residents' lives and make the city more eco-friendly. As a result of the Trust's work, many residents now have jobs growing food and collecting waste for the community.

Ivory Park also now recycles water. Some houses have systems to collect rainwater, so that it is not wasted. Grey water from homes is recycled for use in gardens. More than a dozen people have been trained in water recycling, and it is now their job to train their fellow residents.

GREEN SPACES

Eco-cities are designed so that humans and nature can co-exist. Green spaces, such as parks and gardens, are an important part of an eco-city.

WHY GREEN SPACES MATTER

Trees and other plants absorb CO_2 from the air, which helps in the fight against global warming. The unpaved ground in green spaces also absorbs rainwater, which helps to avoid flooding. And parks provide somewhere for local wildlife to live.

Green spaces are also important for an eco-city's residents. Scientists have shown that when people have access to green spaces, they are more likely to be active. This helps to improve their health, which in turn makes people happier.

GREEN CITIES

Some cities have a lot more green space per person than others:

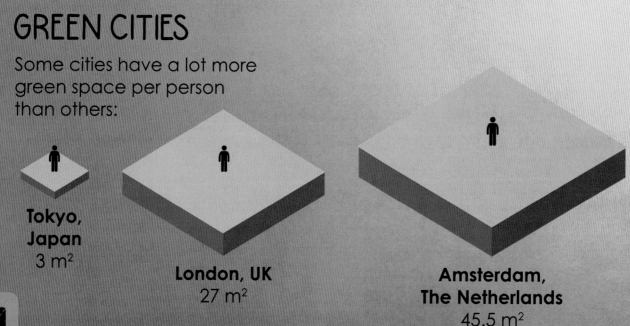

Tokyo, Japan
3 m^2

London, UK
27 m^2

Amsterdam, The Netherlands
45.5 m^2

About 5 million people visit the High Line every year.

GARDEN IN THE SKY

The High Line was an elevated railway track that ran through New York City, USA. For decades it was used by freight trains, but in 1980 it was abandoned. Local residents thought it would make a great park. It took a while, but in 2009 the first section was opened.

The High Line is now a corridor of green space that runs for over two kilometres through Manhattan. It is home to more than 200 types of plants, which have attracted birds, bees and other wildlife. There are walking paths and sculptures for visitors to enjoy, too.

LOCAL FOOD

Eco-cities try to make use of local food, because most food is transported in vehicles that use fossil fuels. Food from nearby doesn't have to travel so far, so releases less CO_2.

THE CLOSER, THE BETTER

Big supermarket chains get their food from wherever they can buy it most cheaply. Sometimes it even comes from another continent. In an eco-city, people are encouraged to support local food producers.

There may be small supermarkets that get food from nearby growers. Or residents can buy fruit, vegetables, flowers and meat at farmers' markets. The food they sell is often fresher, as well as being more eco-friendly.

FOOD MILES

In the USA, on average, food travels ...

2,400 kilometres

... from farm to plate.

Non-local food transport creates up to ...

17 x as much CO_2

... as local food.

When food is transported long distances, a lot of carbon dioxide is released.

COMMUNITY GARDEN

In Berkhamsted, England, a local council and a charity have teamed up to start a community garden. It is part of an activity centre that helps adults with learning disabilities develop new skills and train for jobs. They are taught how to take care of fruit trees and other plants.

The fruit and vegetables they grow are used to make meals for the workers (so it would be impossible for their meals to be any more local). Any leftover food is turned into jam, chutney or juice, which is sold in the farm shop.

As an added bonus, members of the public are welcome to walk through the orchard and enjoy the relaxing green space.

City gardens give people who live in flats the chance to grow their own food.

CITIES OF THE FUTURE

More than 4 billion people now live in cities, and the biggest cities have populations of more than 20 million people.

CHANGING OUR CITIES

It wouldn't be practical to abandon our existing cities and move to new eco-cities, built from scratch. Instead, cities need to constantly change and evolve. New buildings have to be more energy efficient. Public transport needs to work well and use renewable energy.

Some of the world's greenest cities, such as Freiburg in Germany, are fairly small. But cities of every size, from small to giant, can make changes to reduce their impact on the planet. And in a giant city of 20 million people, even small changes can add up to make a big difference!

WORLD POPULATION

1980
4.4 billion

2015
7.3 billion

2050
9.7 billion
(predicted)

As the population increases, many more people will live in cities.

Treasure Island residents will get amazing views, along with eco-friendly living.

ECO-ISLAND

In 2011, San Francisco officials approved plans for a whole new eco-town to be built on two small islands in San Francisco Bay. They are Treasure Island, a former naval base, and neighbouring Yerba Buena Island. The eco-town will have 8,000 homes, as well as hotels, restaurants, shops and offices.

A ferry terminal will connect the eco-town to San Francisco, but residents will be able to get most of what they need without leaving. There will be green spaces, a school and even an organic farm. Energy will be solar- and wind-powered. The town has been designed so that every home is within a 10-minute walk of all basic goods.

GLOSSARY

atmosphere a layer of gases that surrounds the Earth

carbon dioxide a gas produced by burning some types of fuel. When it builds up in the atmosphere, it traps the Sun's heat

carbon footprint the amount of carbon dioxide and other harmful gases that are released

climate change the gradual change in the Earth's climate, brought about by global warming

compost to turn plant waste into fertiliser by letting it decay

emission something that is released into the atmosphere, such as exhaust fumes from a car

fossil fuels oil, coal, and natural gas, which are formed from the long-dead remains of living things

fuel anything that can be burned as a source of energy

global warming the gradual warming of the Earth's temperature, caused partly by burning fossil fuels

insulation building material used to stop a building heating up in summer and cooling down in winter

landfill a place where rubbish is buried underground

natural resource material from the natural world that can be used by people

power plant a facility that generates electricity

public transport a system of transportation that is designed to be used by everyone

recycle to treat waste material, so that it can be used again

renewable able to be used without running out

solar panel a flat device that captures sunlight and turns it into electricity, or uses it to heat water

wind turbine a machine with rotating blades that turns wind into electricity